CHINA

PHOTOGRAPHS BY ELIZABETH KRAMER

THIS IS PART OF THE VISITING SERIES.

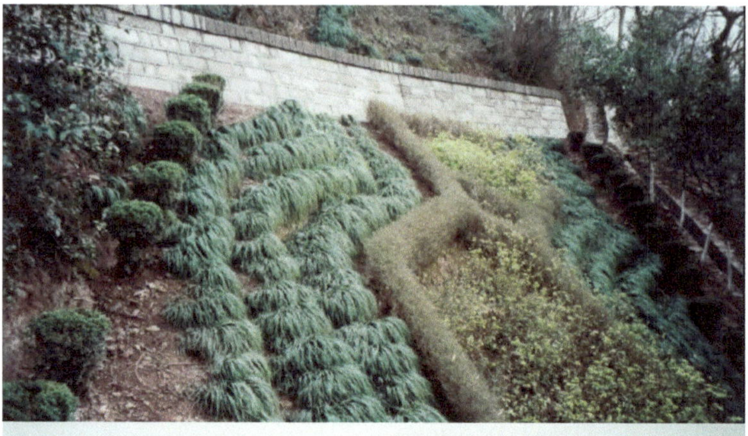
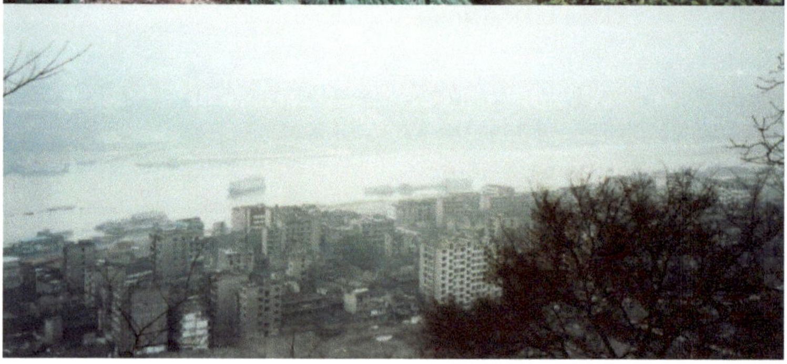

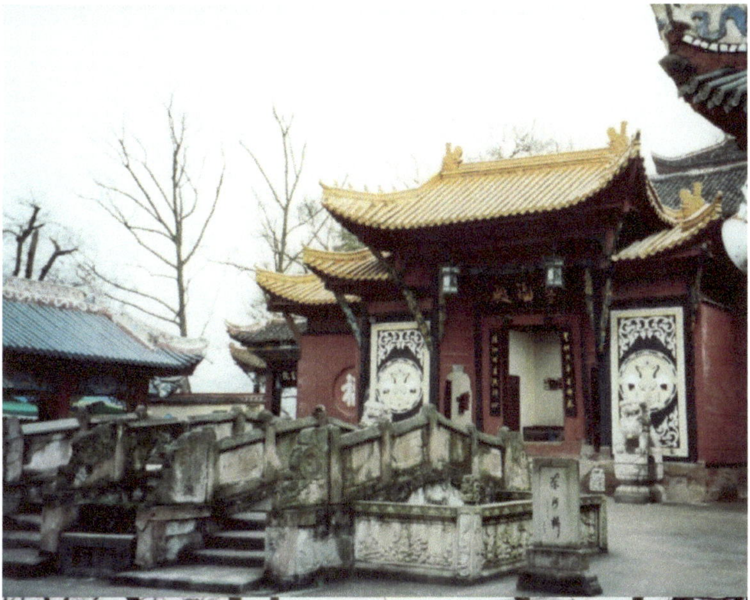

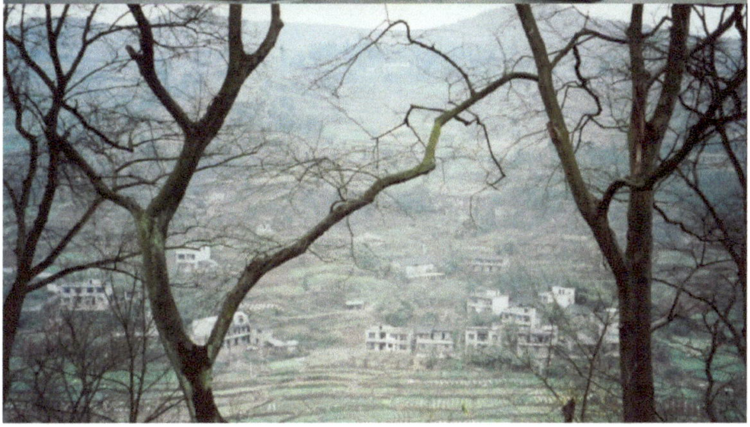

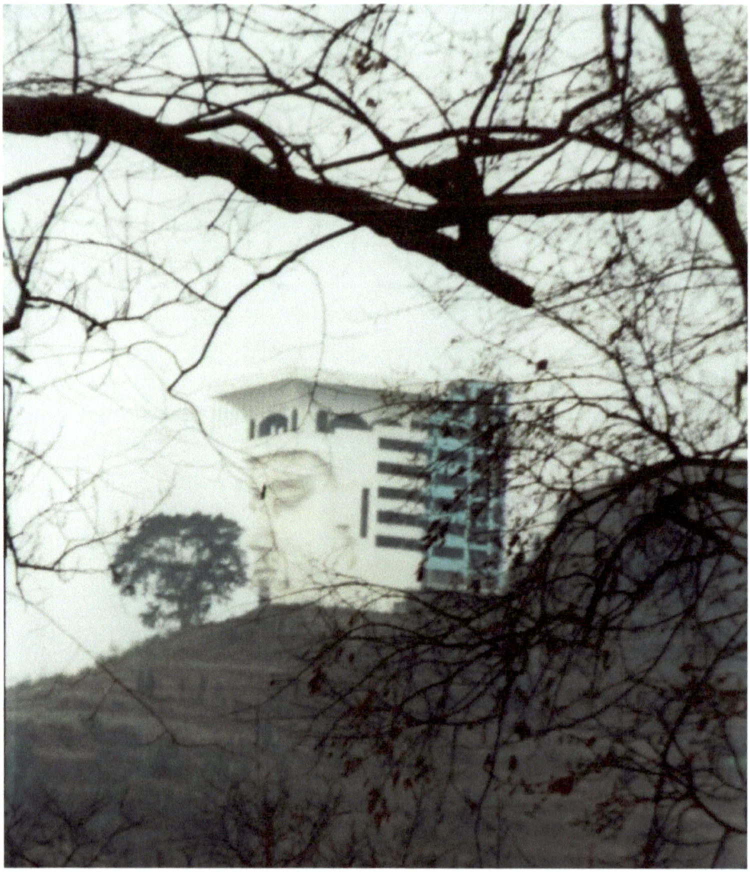

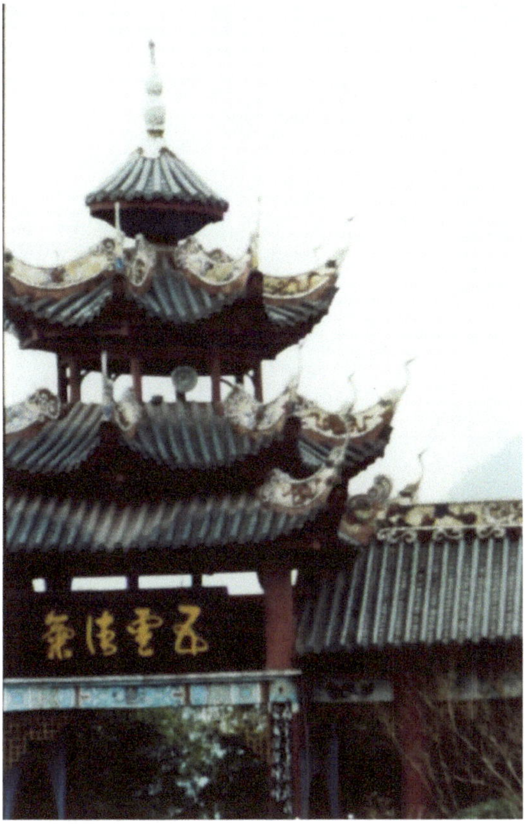

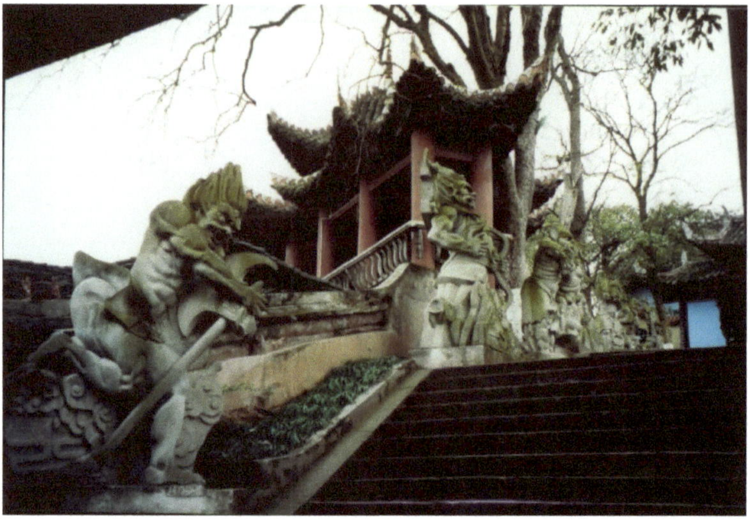

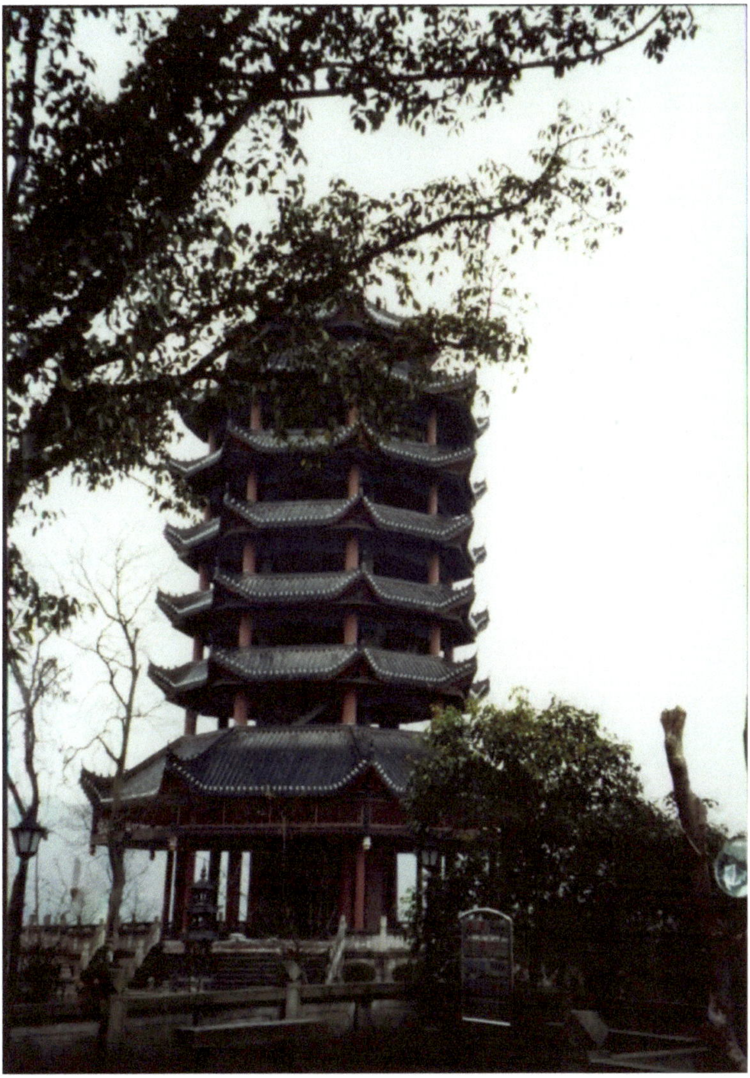

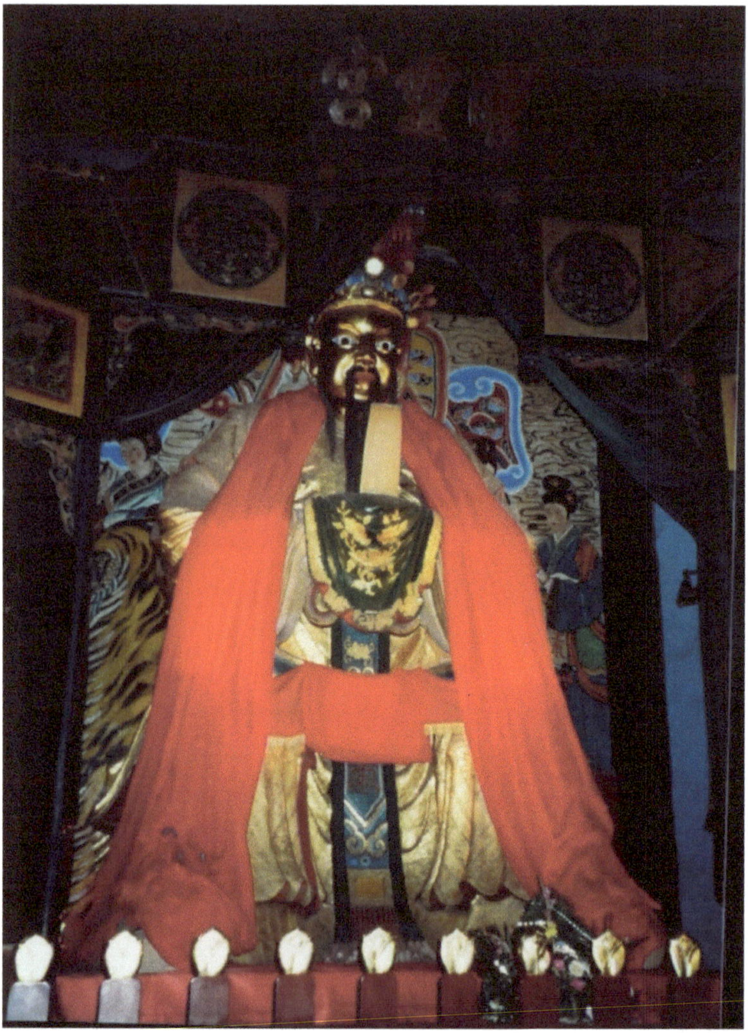

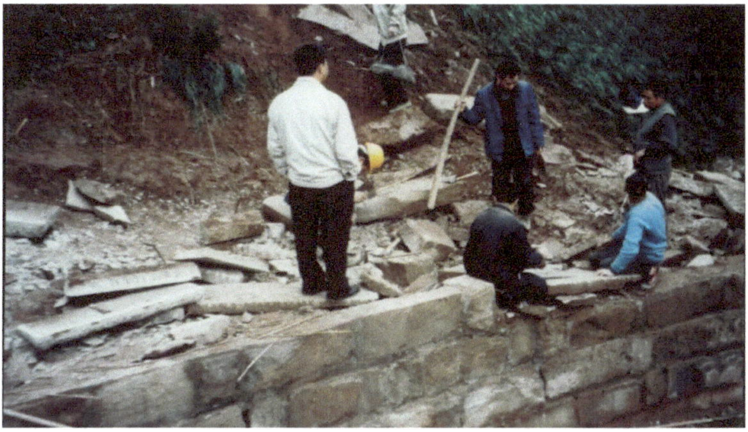

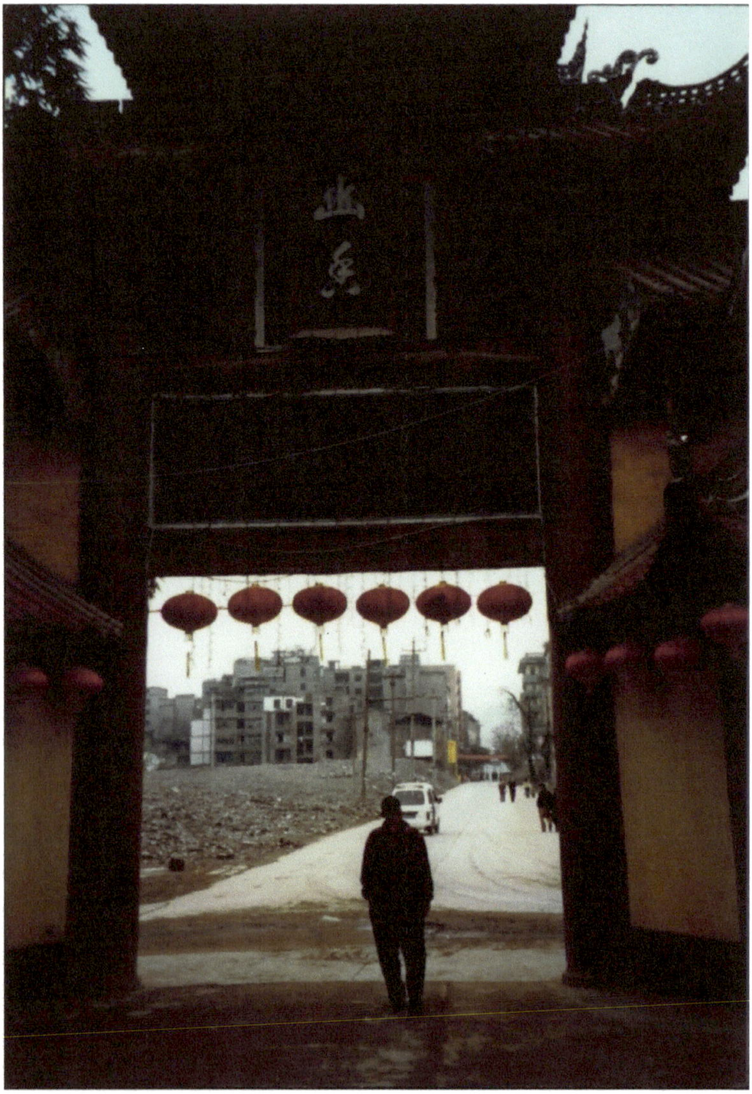

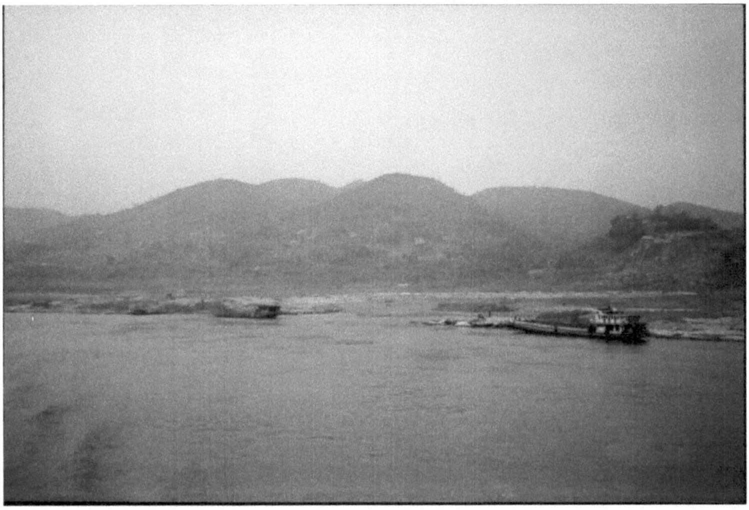

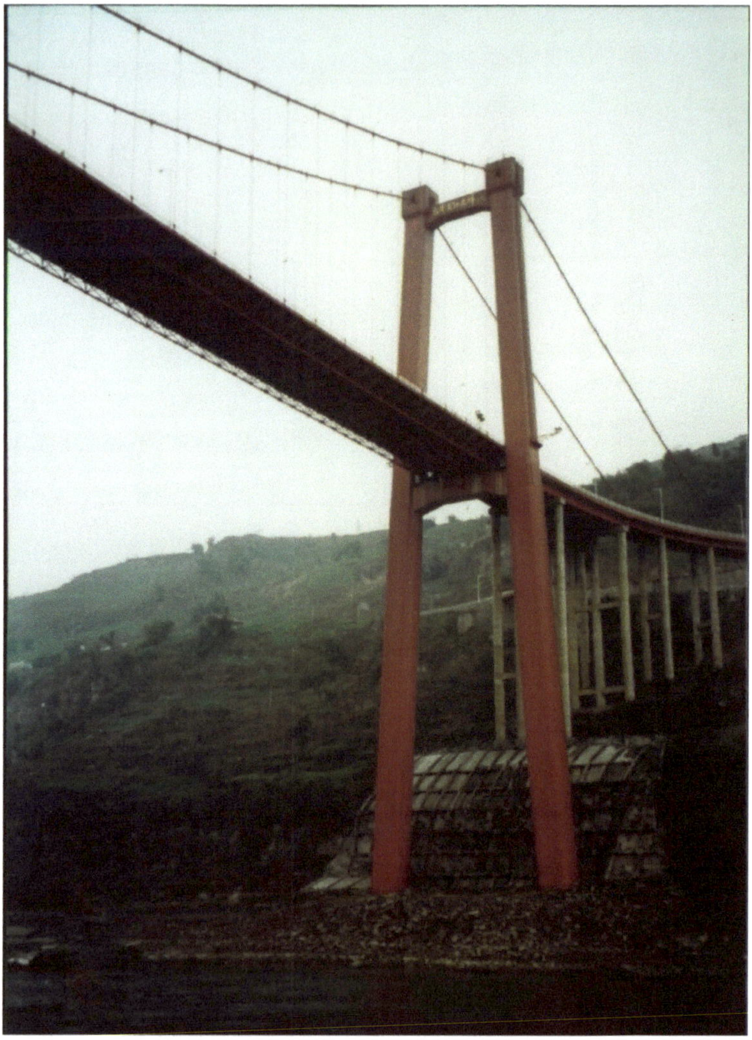

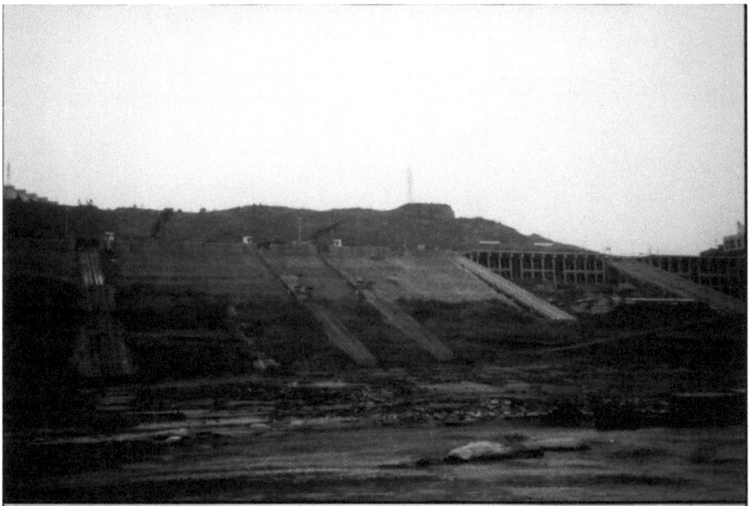

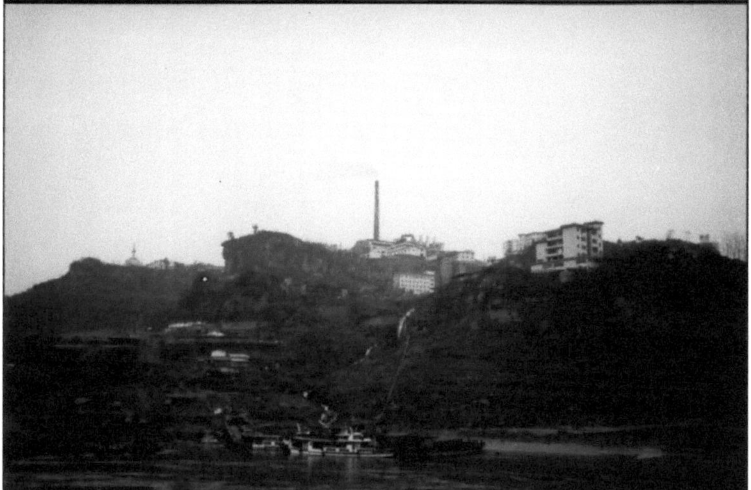

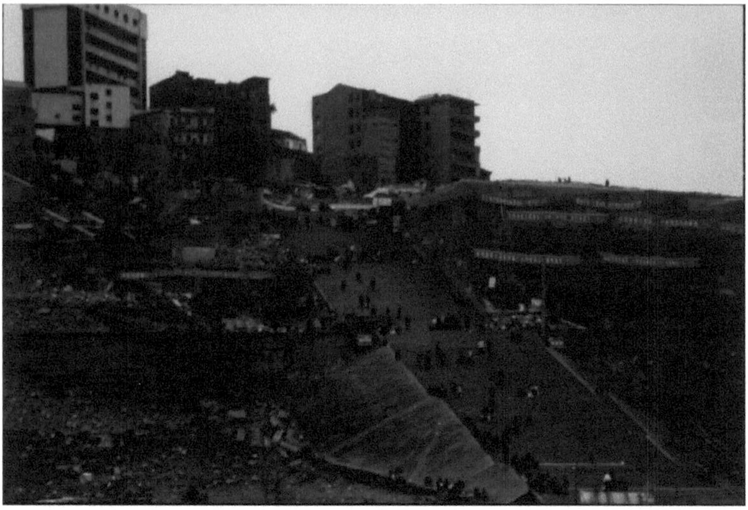

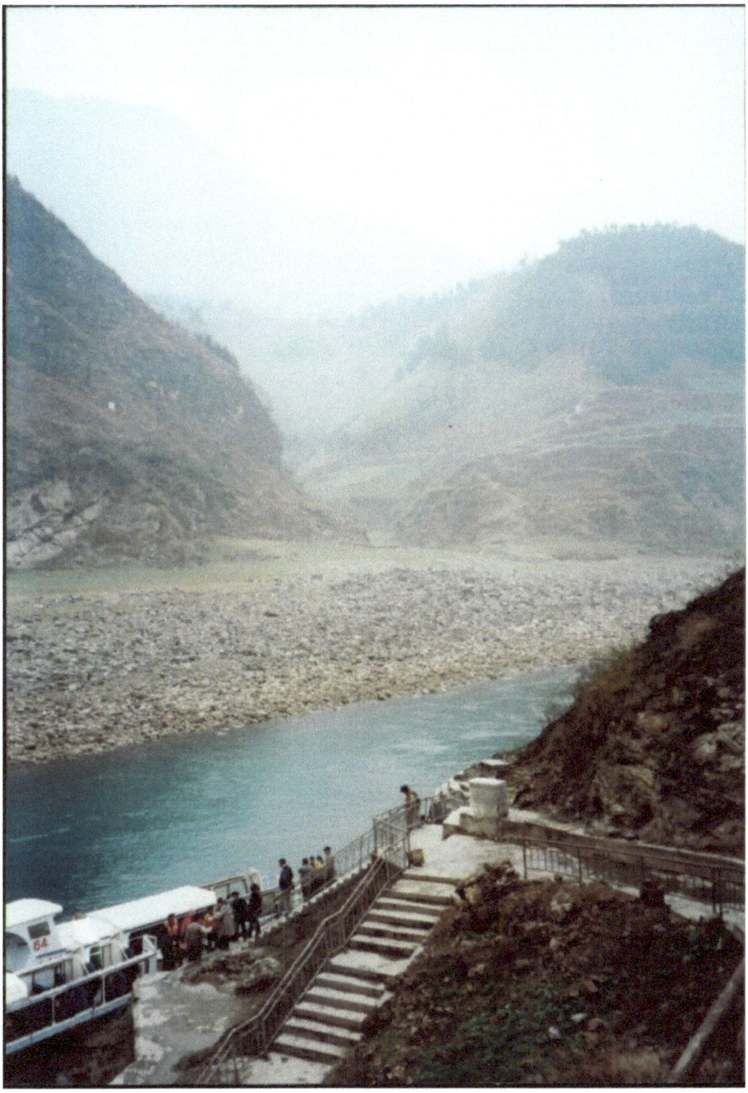

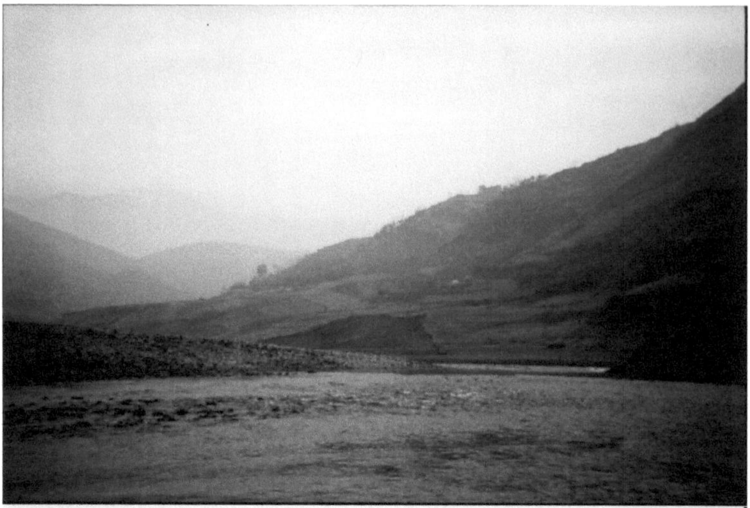
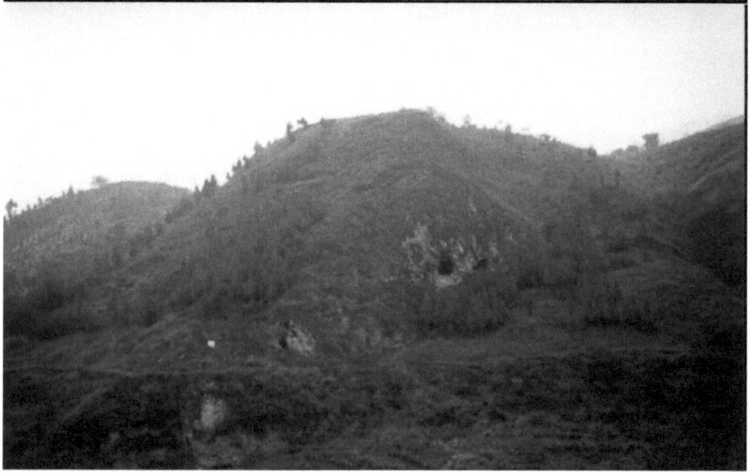

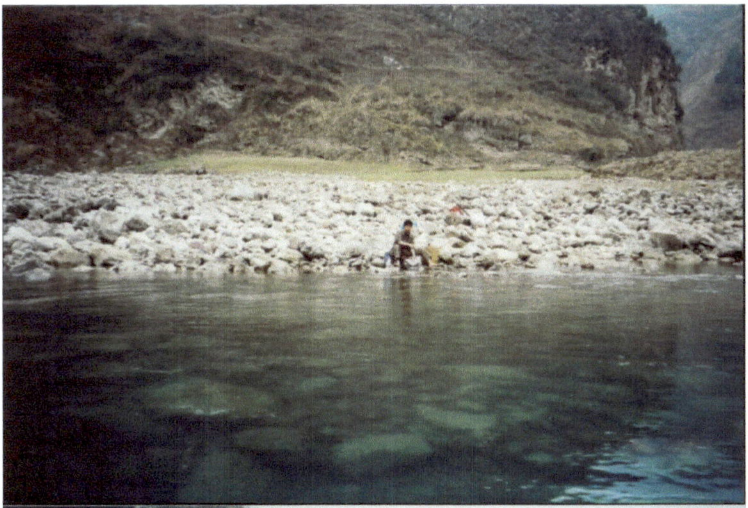

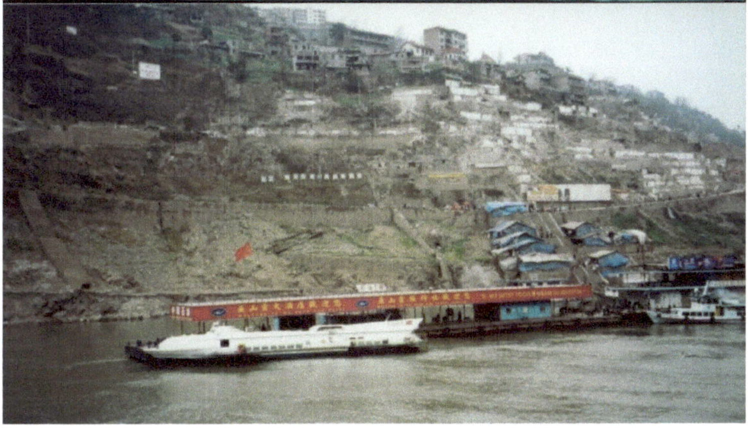

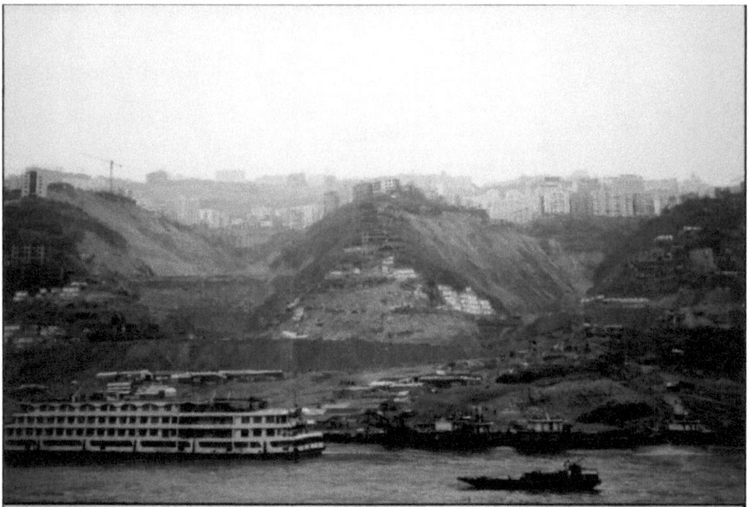

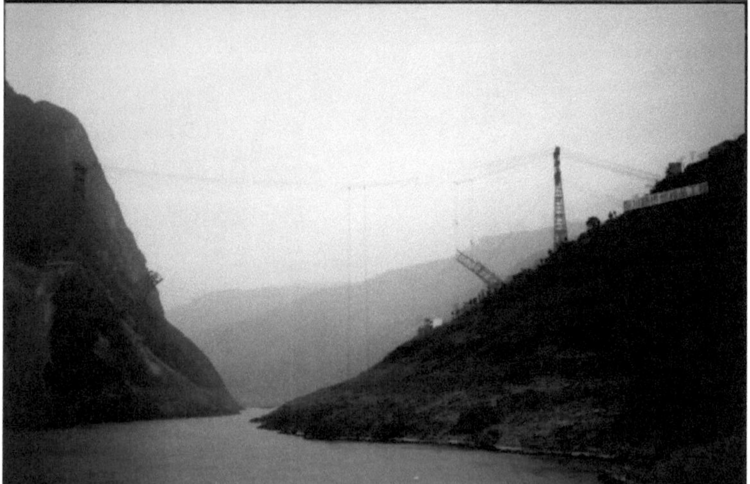

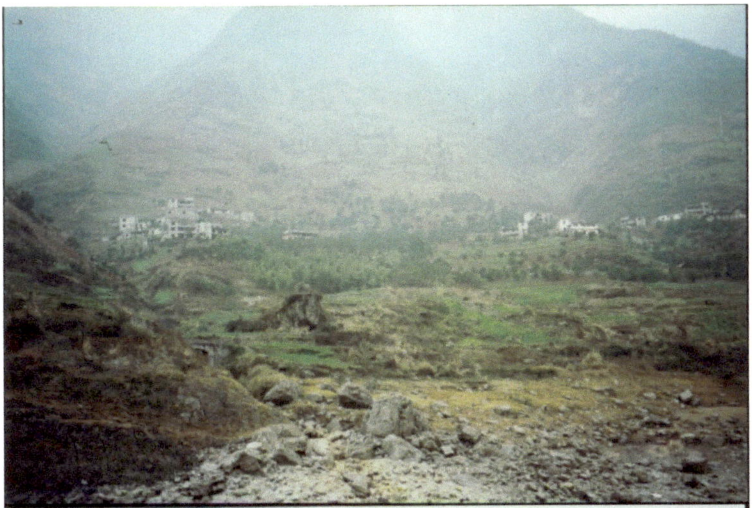

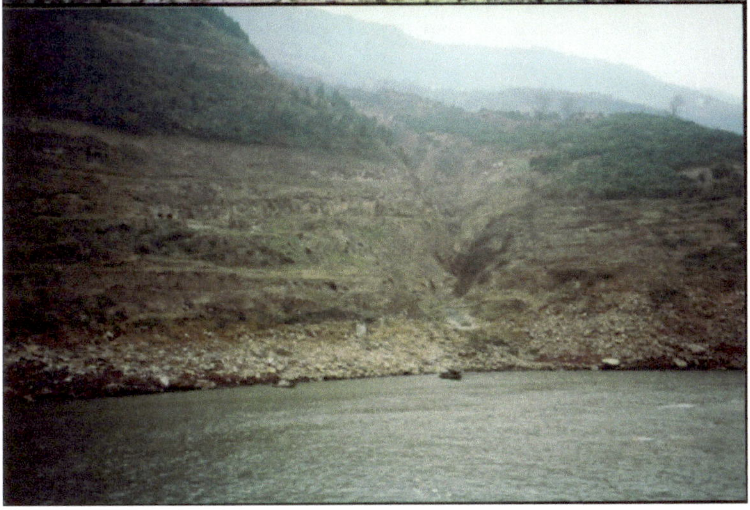

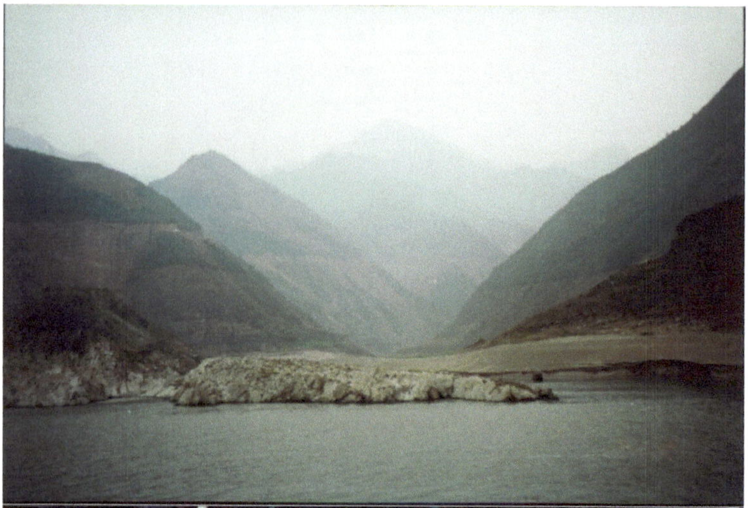

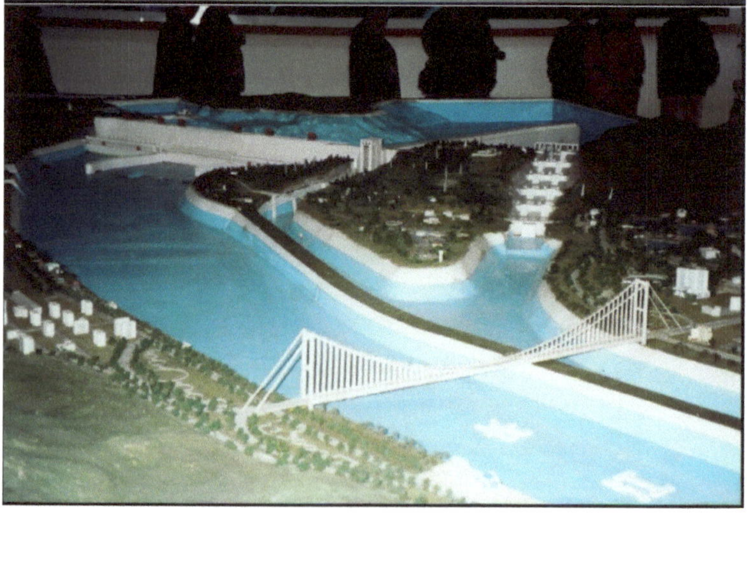

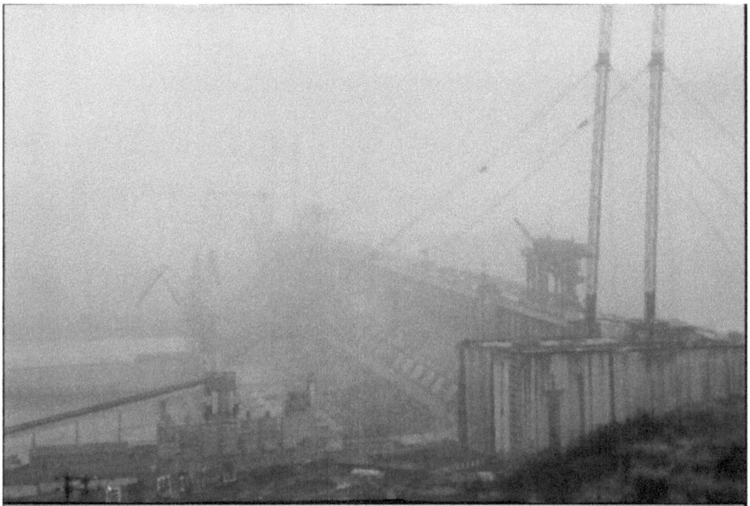

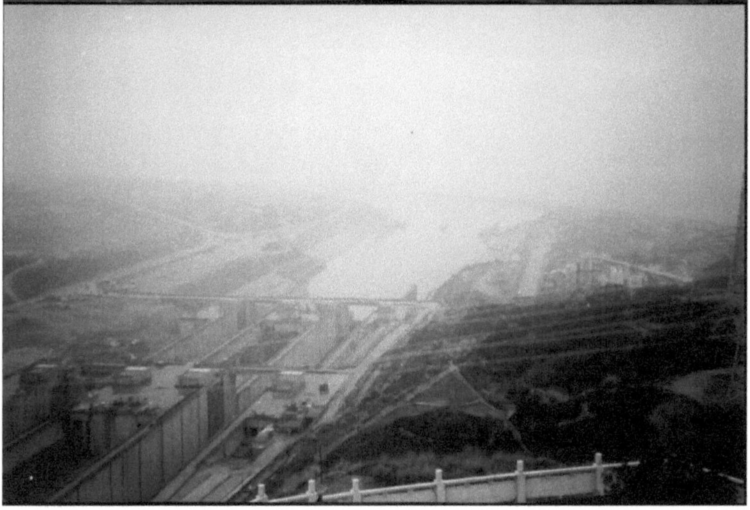

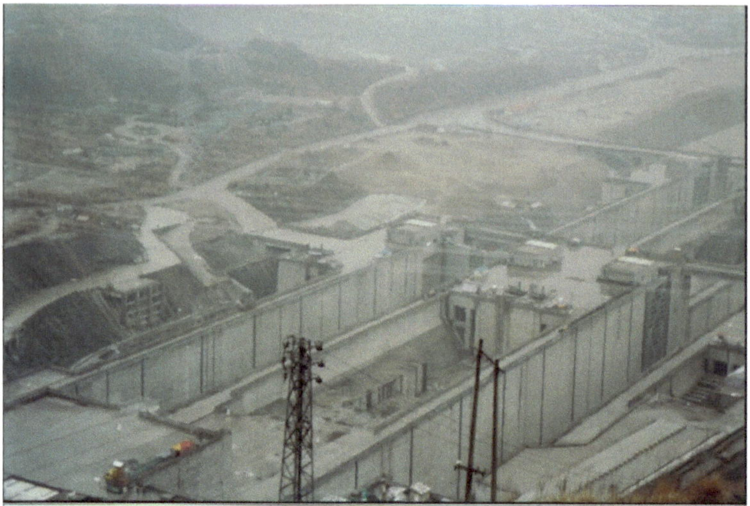
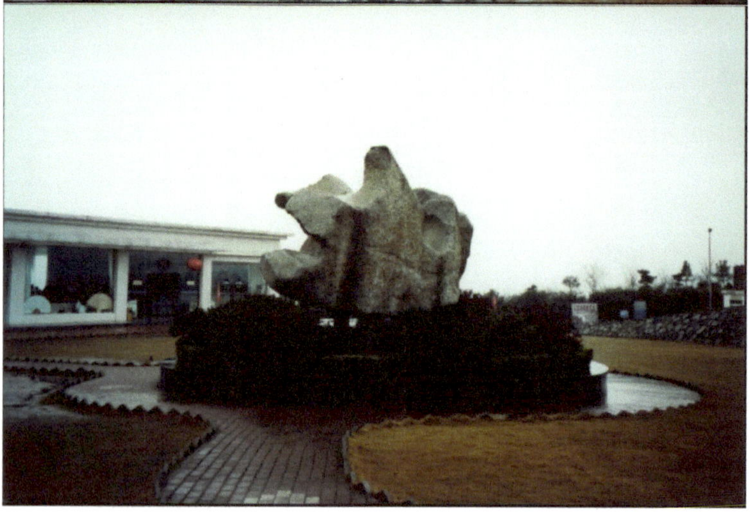

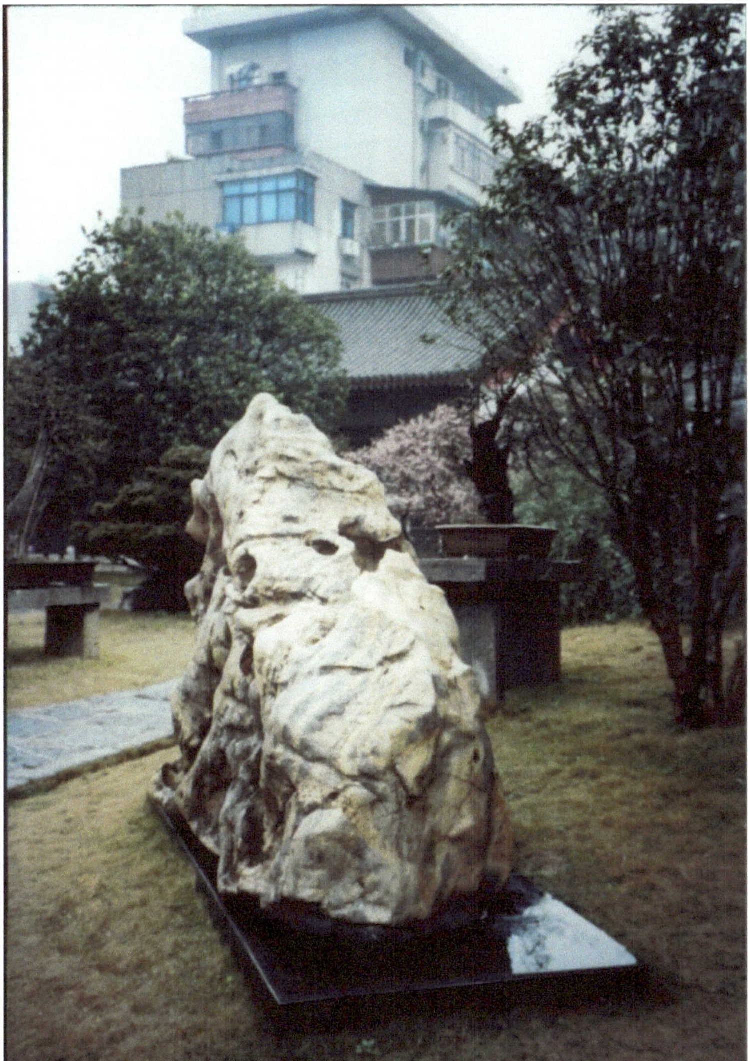

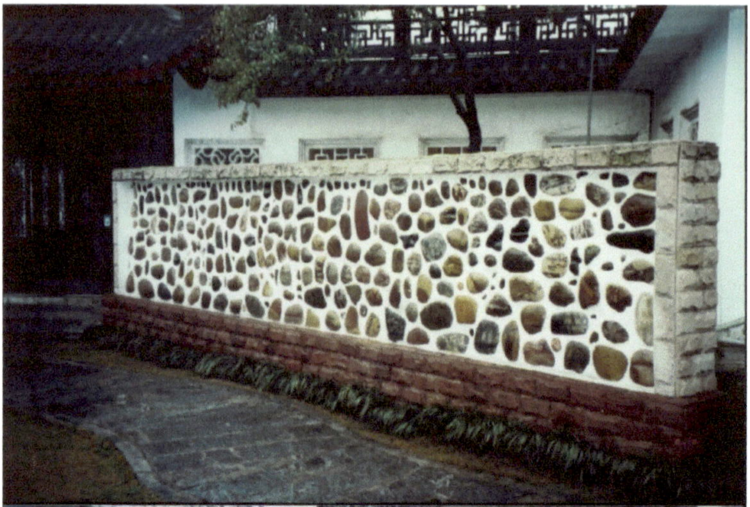

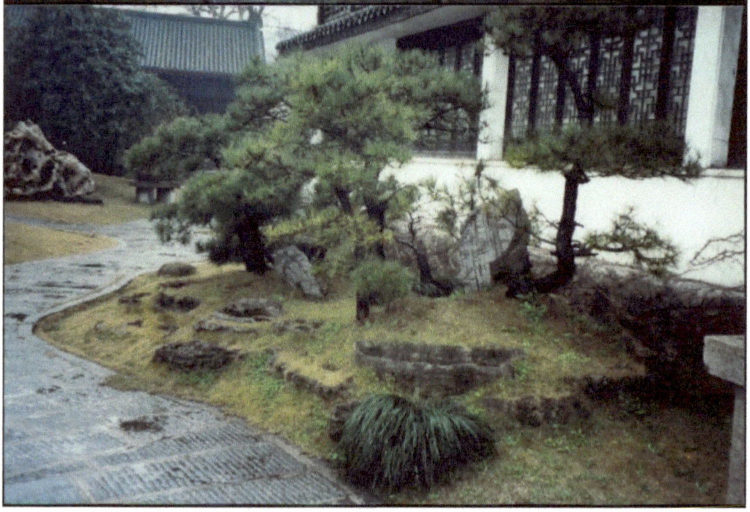

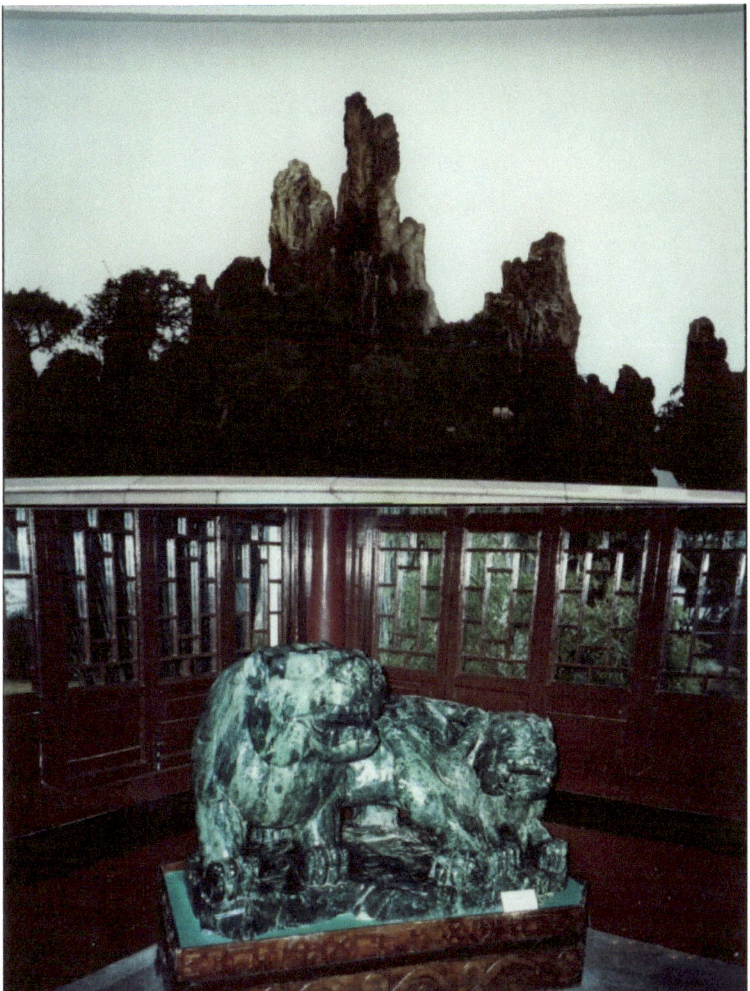

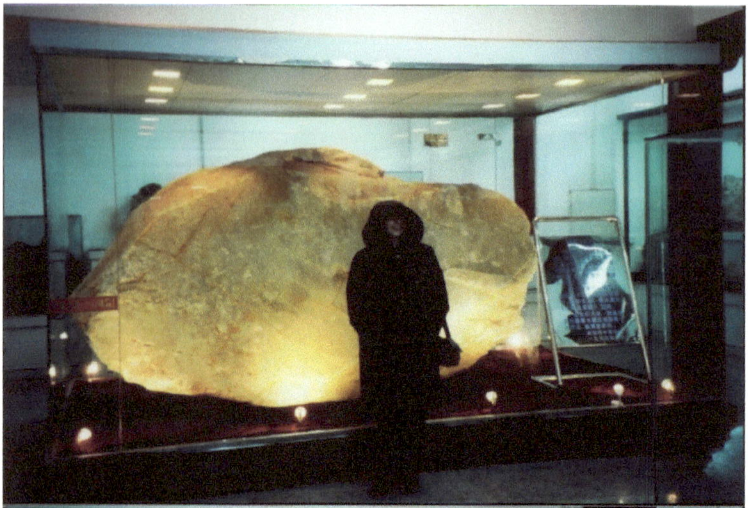

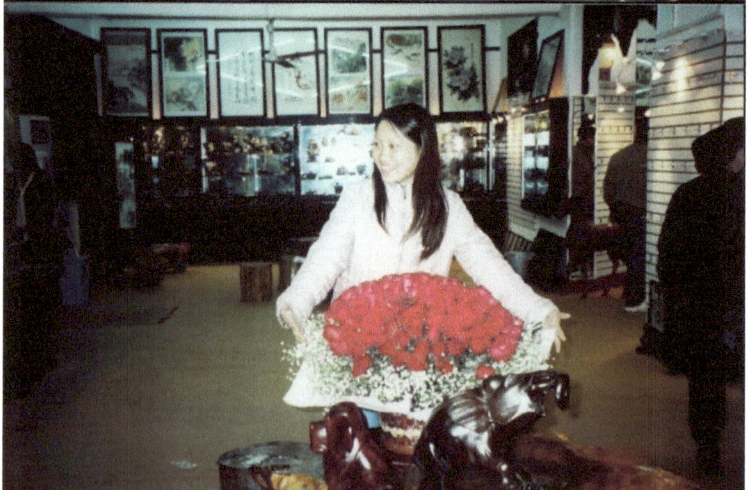

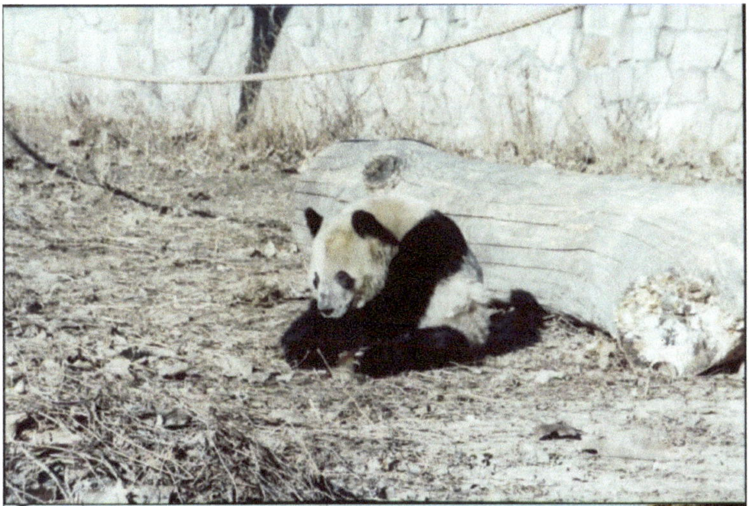

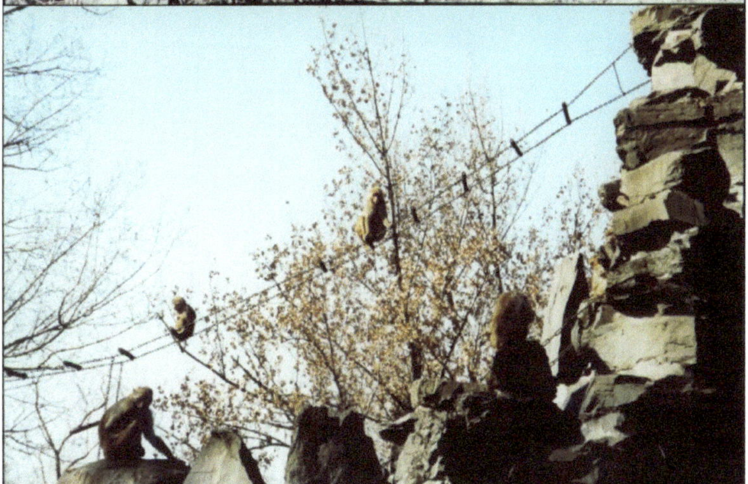

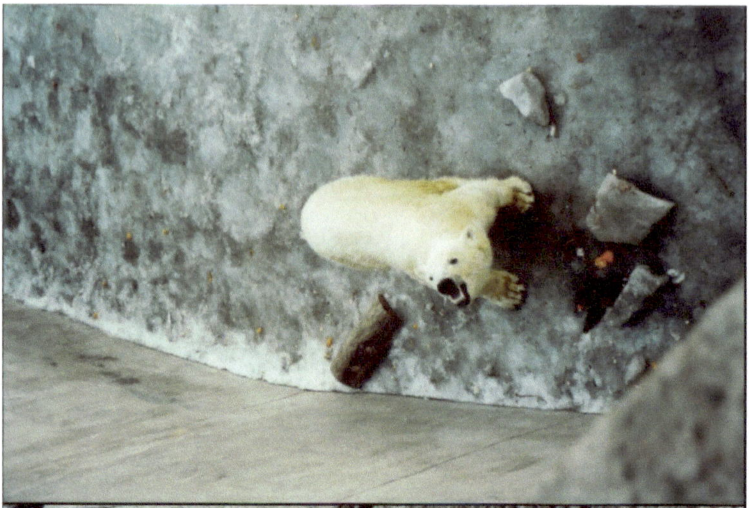

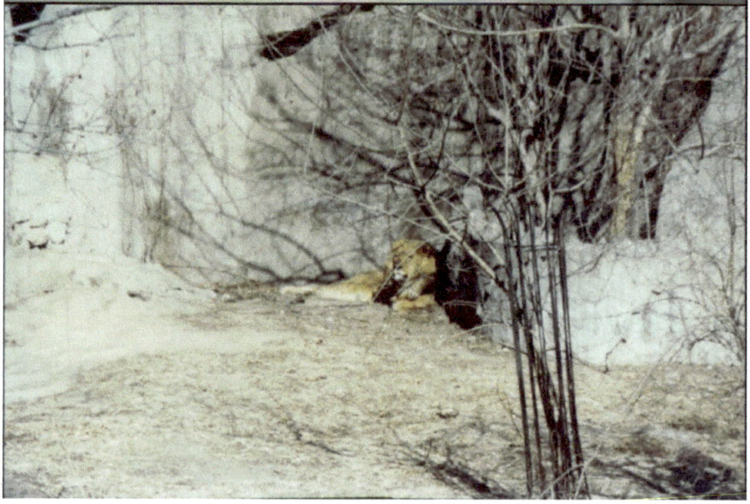

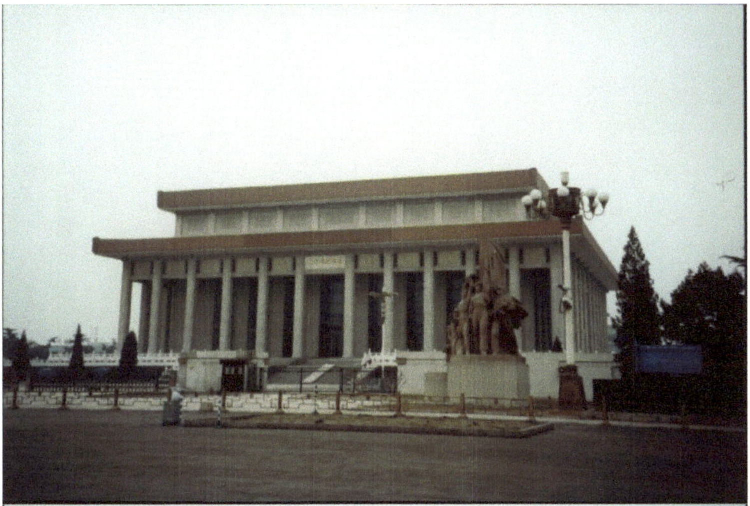

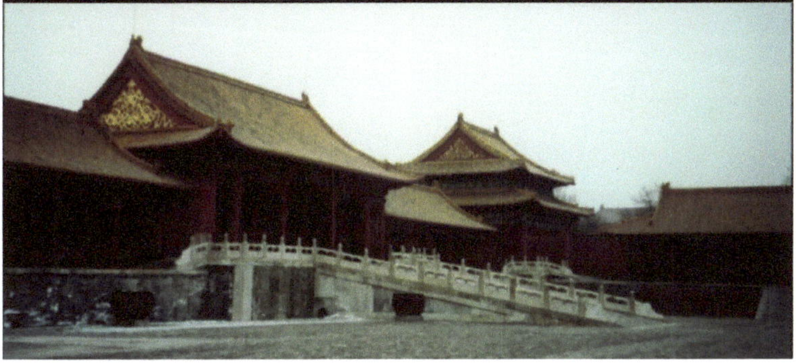

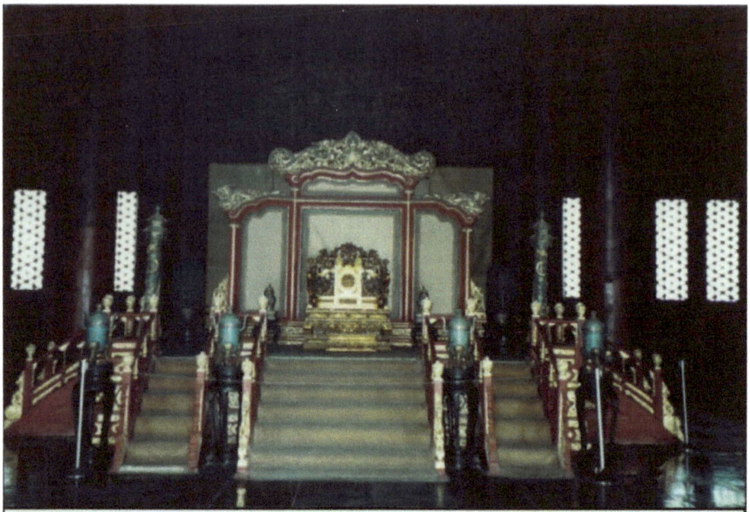

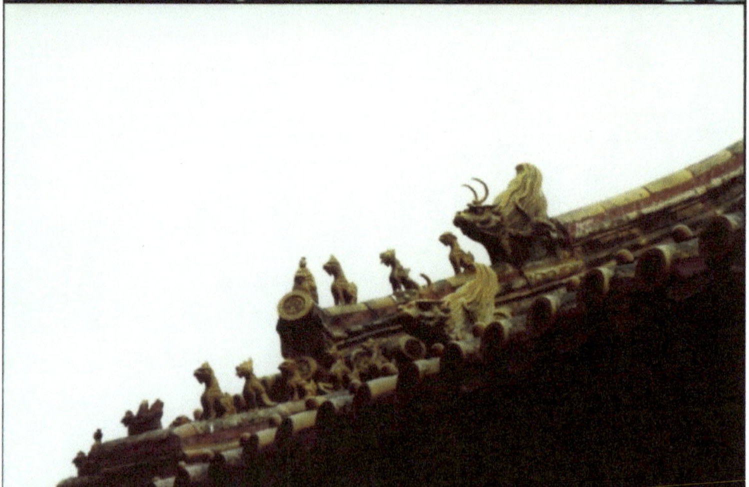

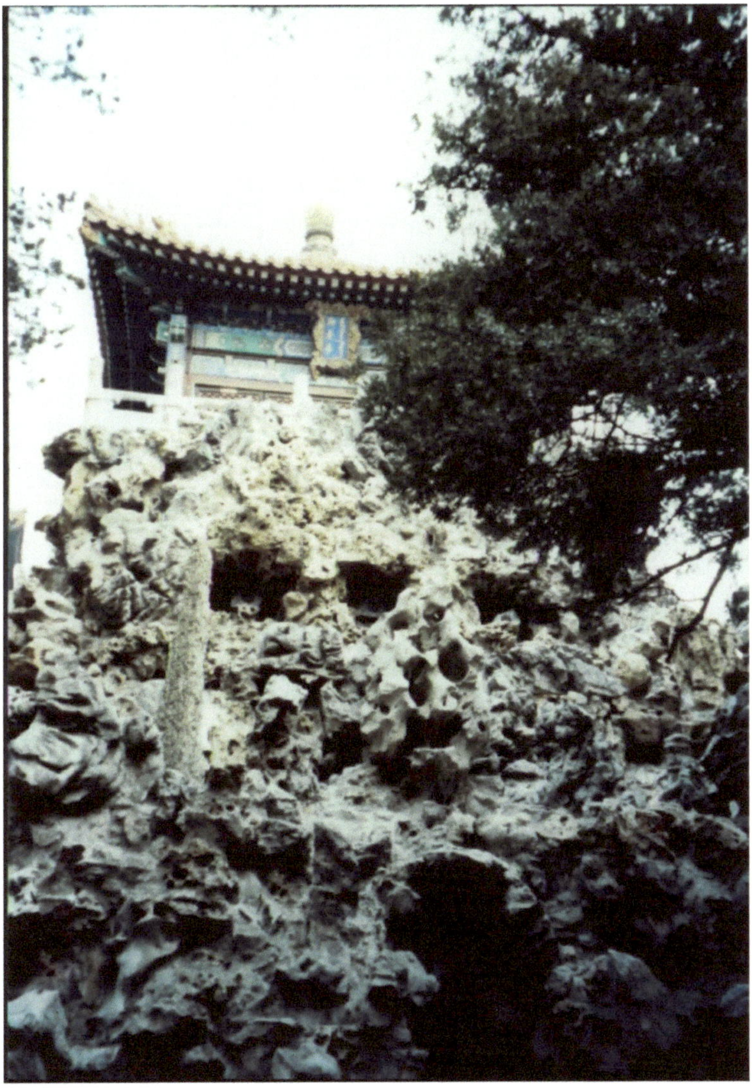

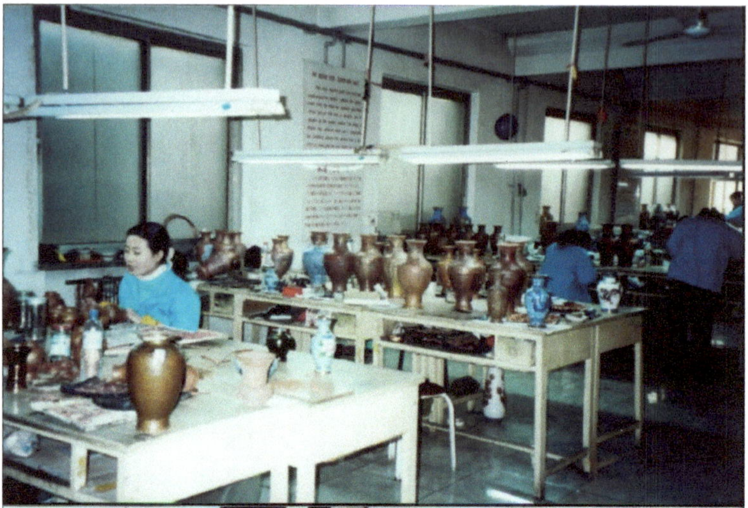

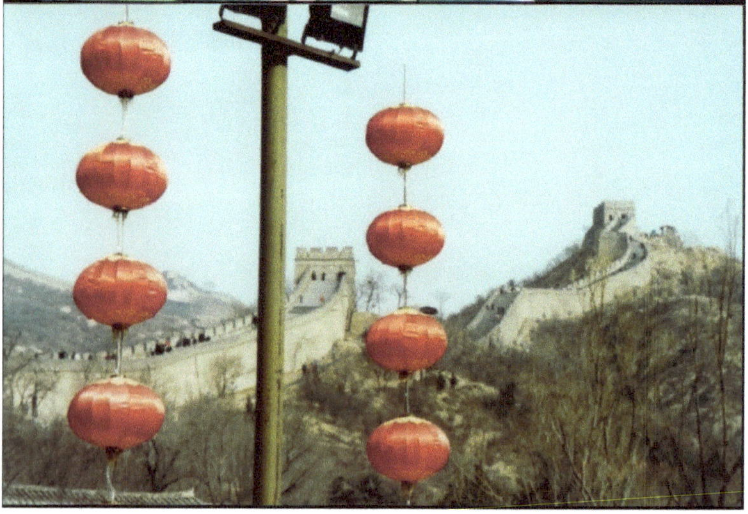

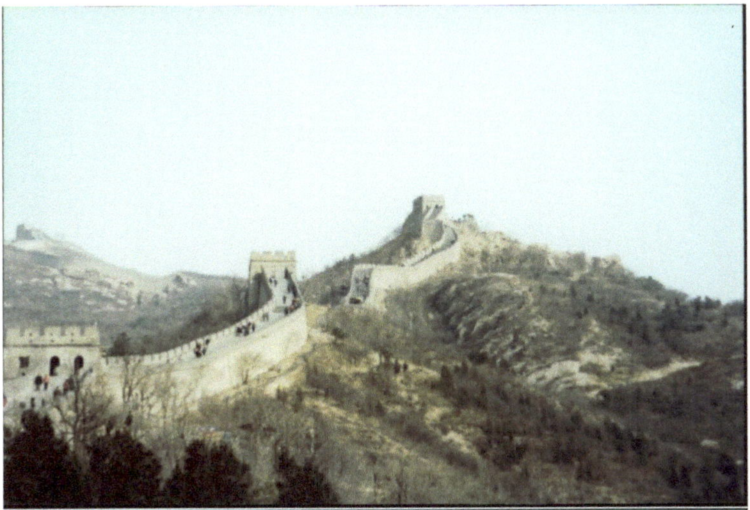

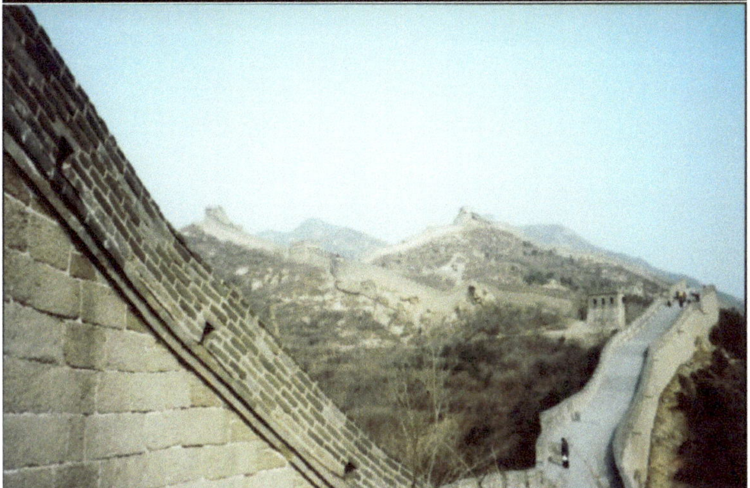

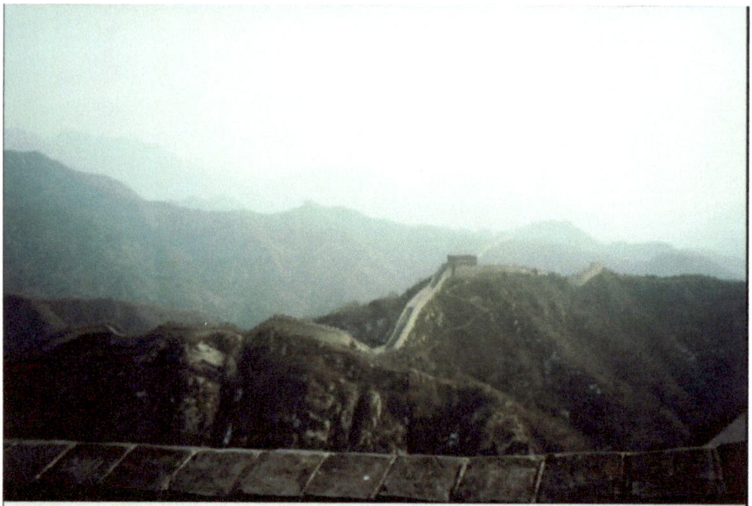

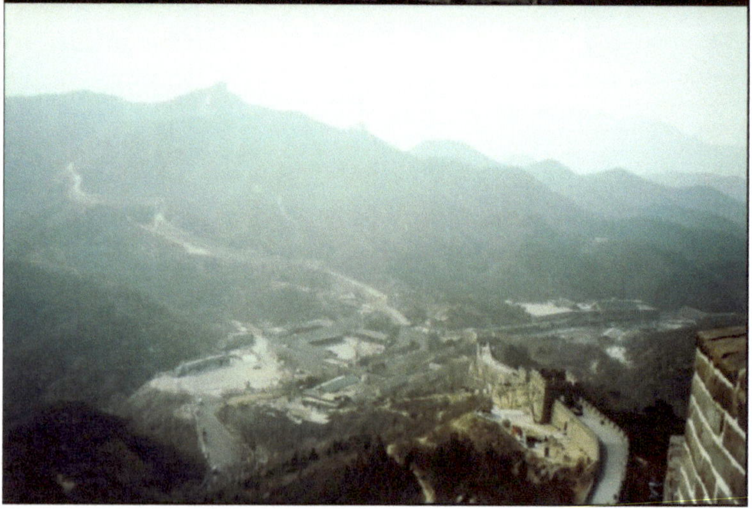

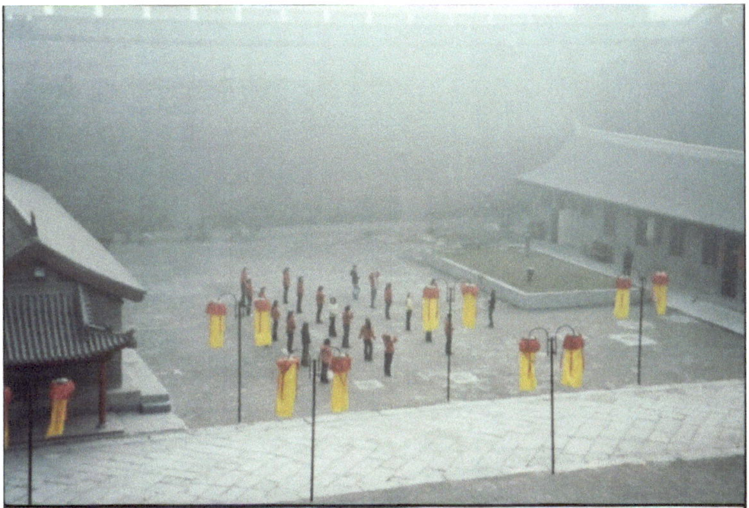

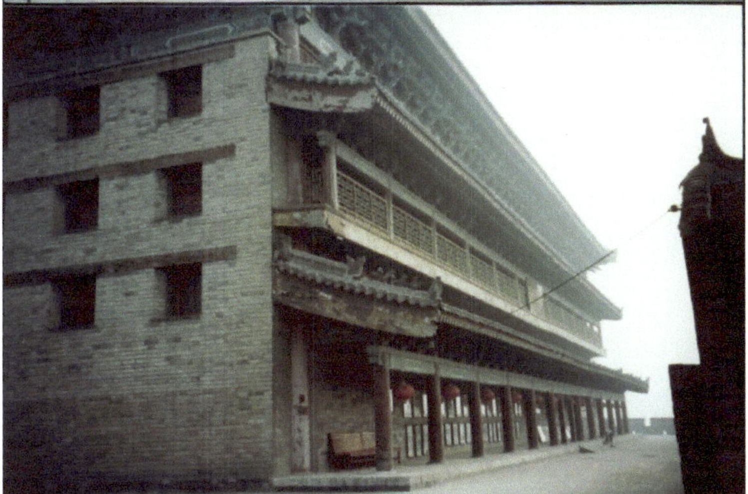

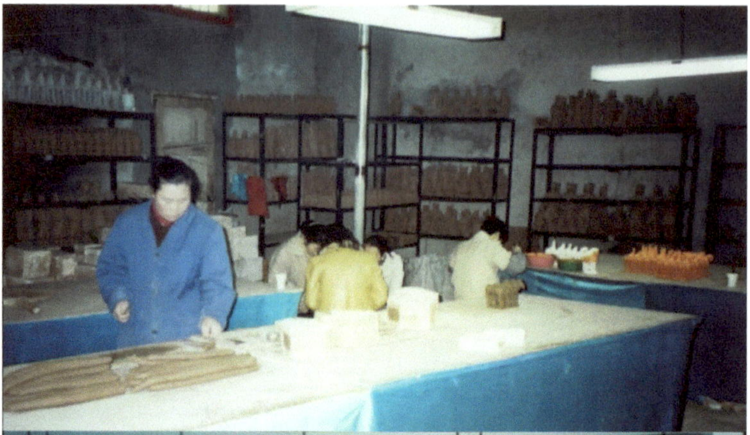

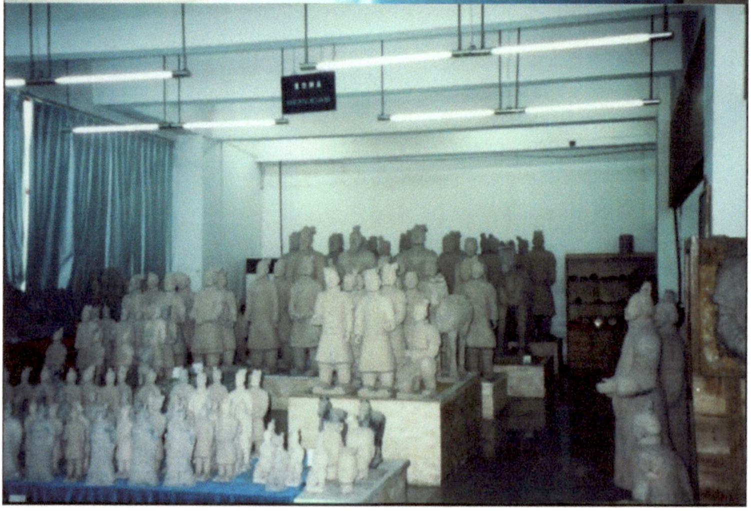

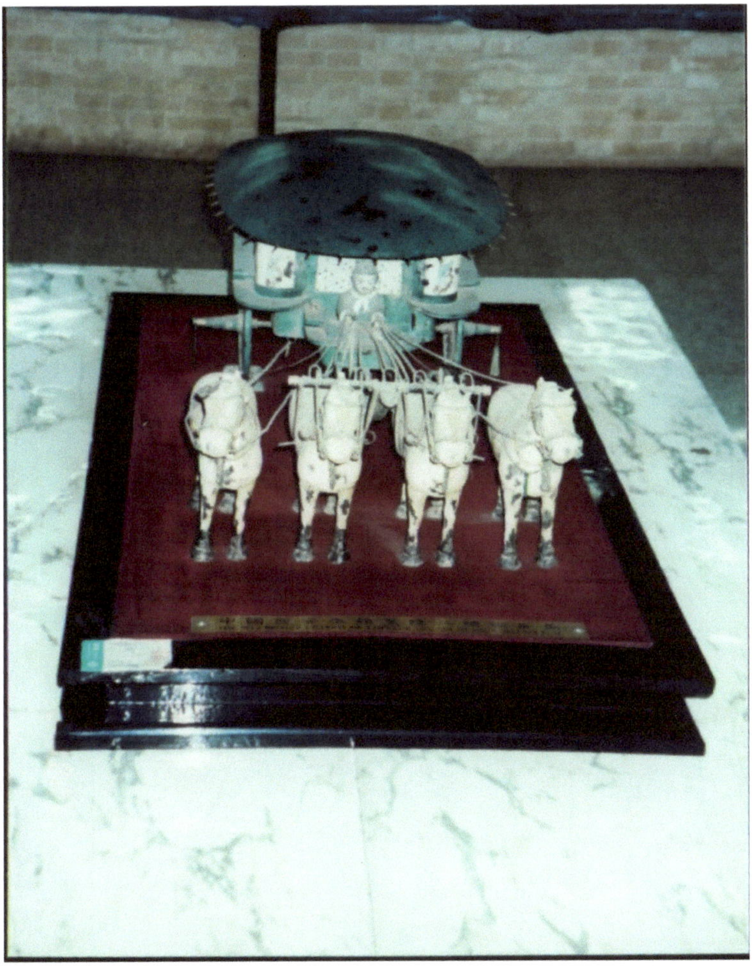

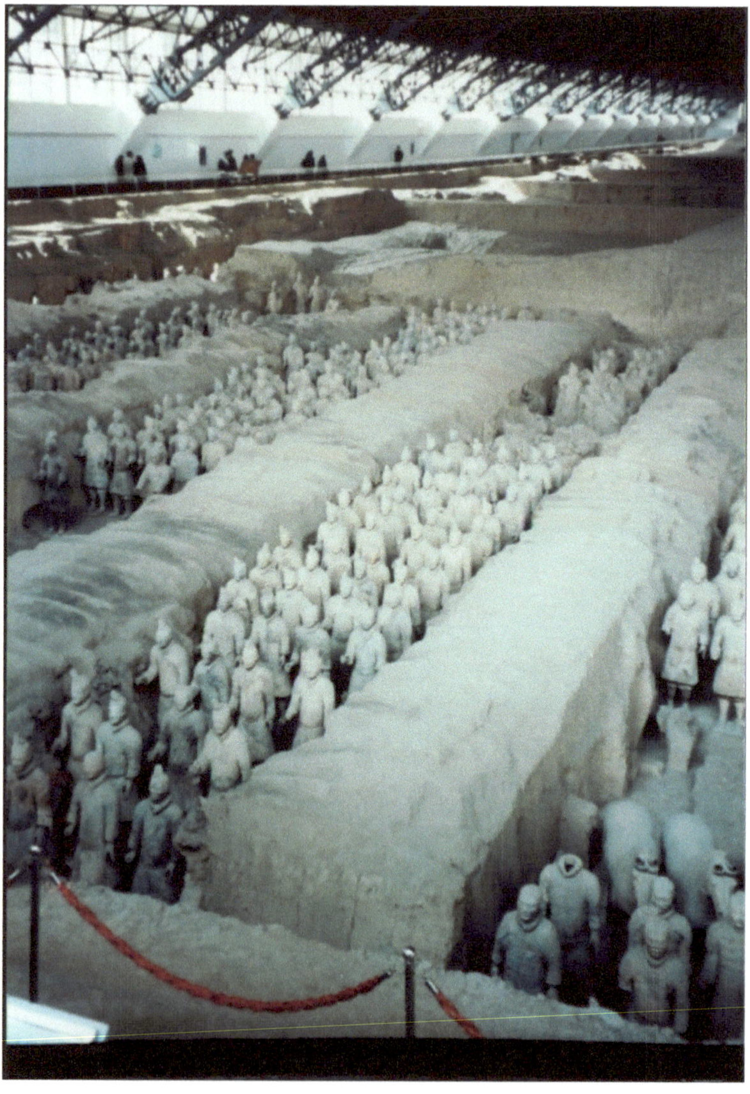

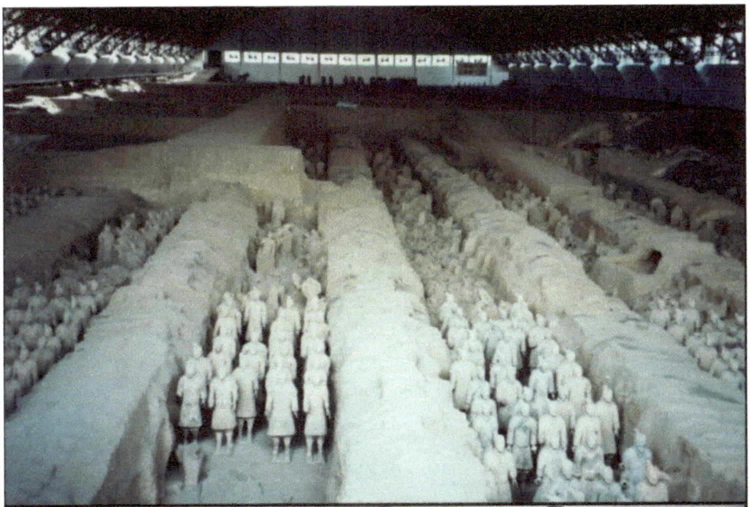

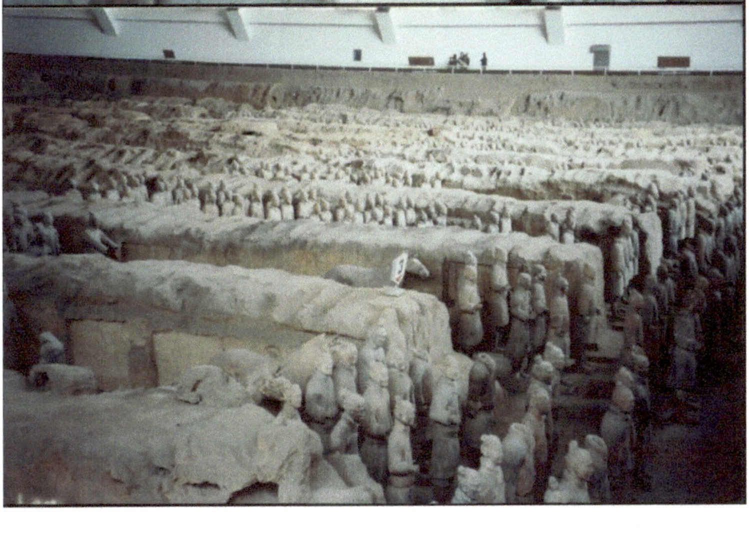

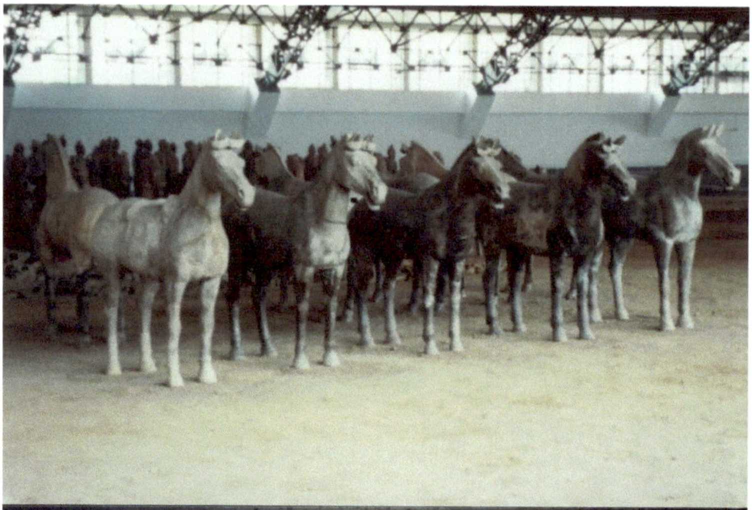

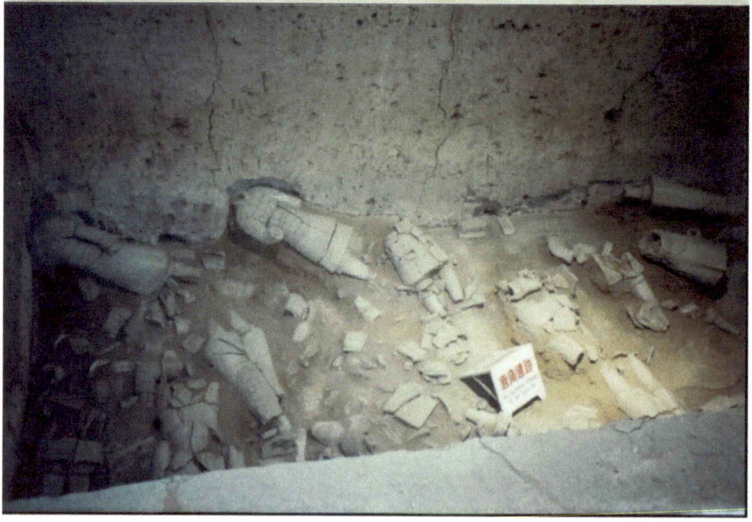

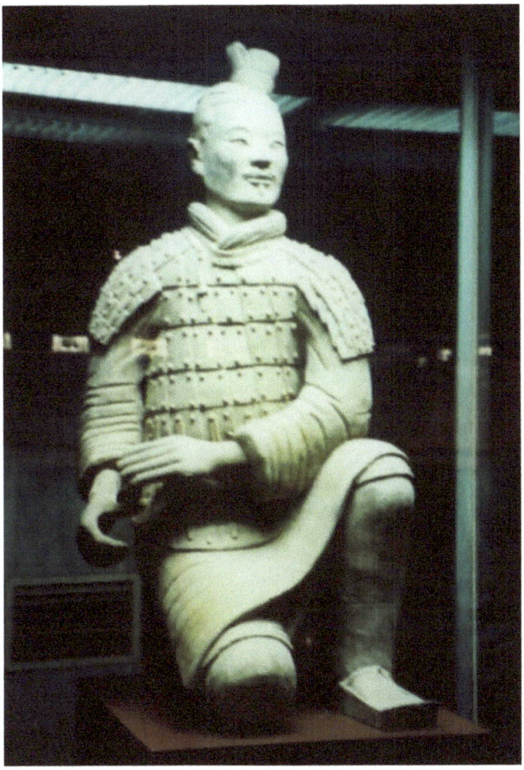

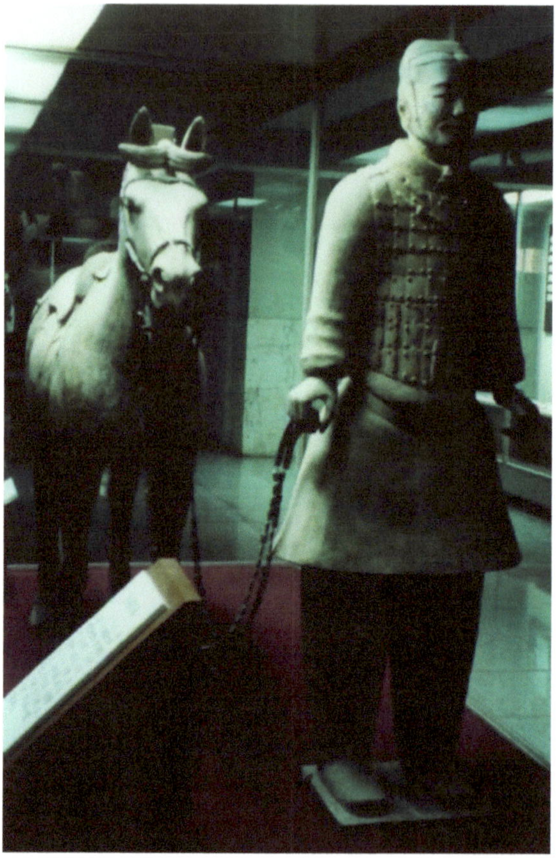

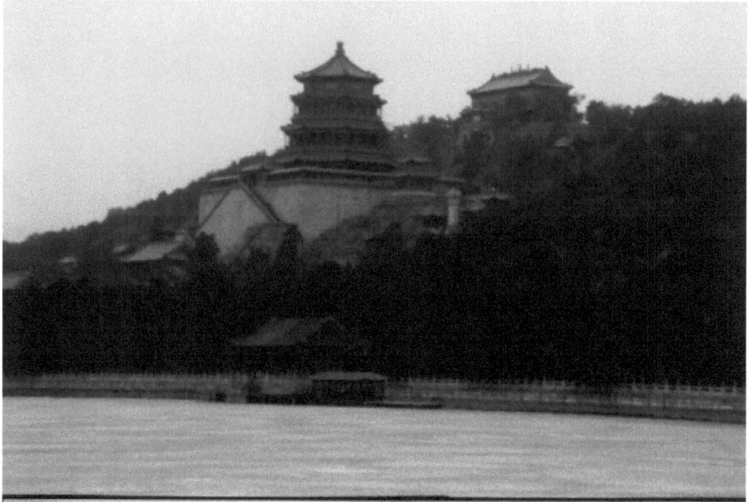

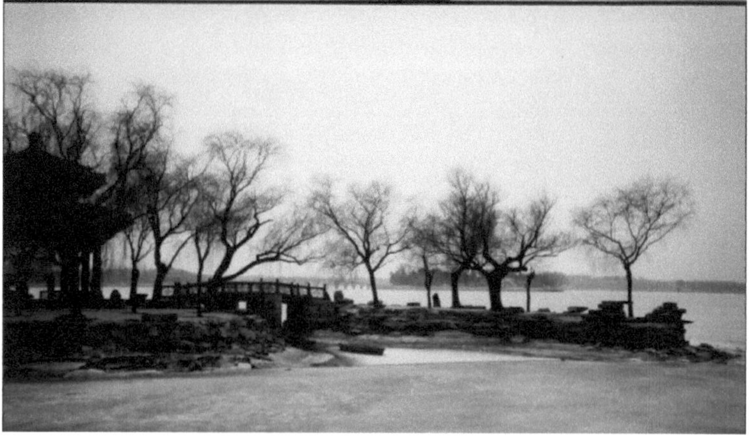

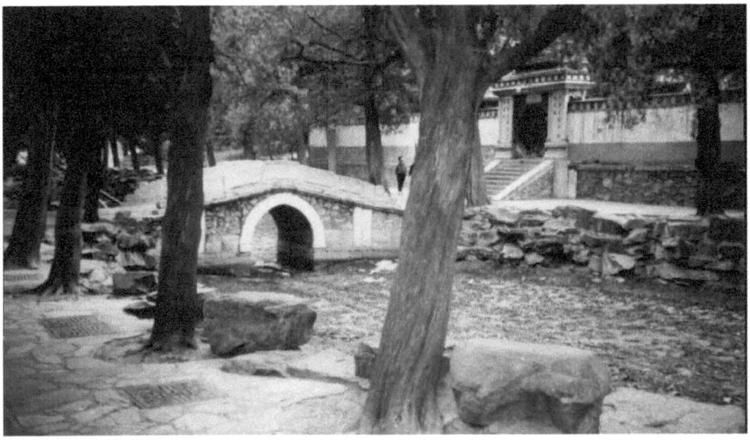

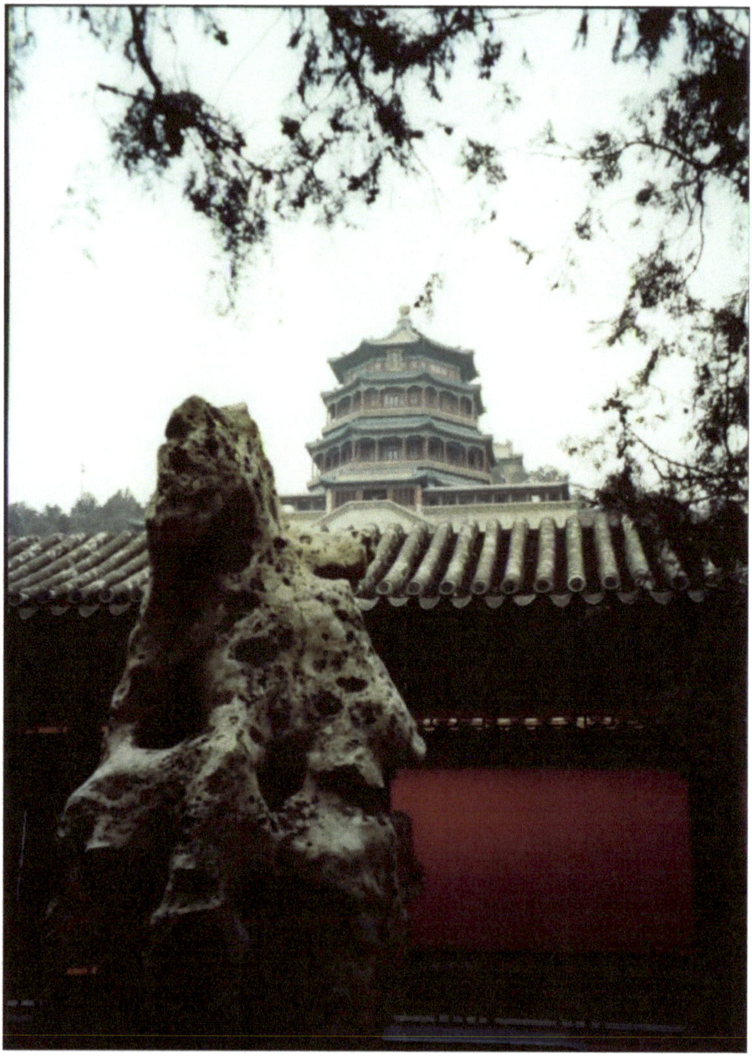

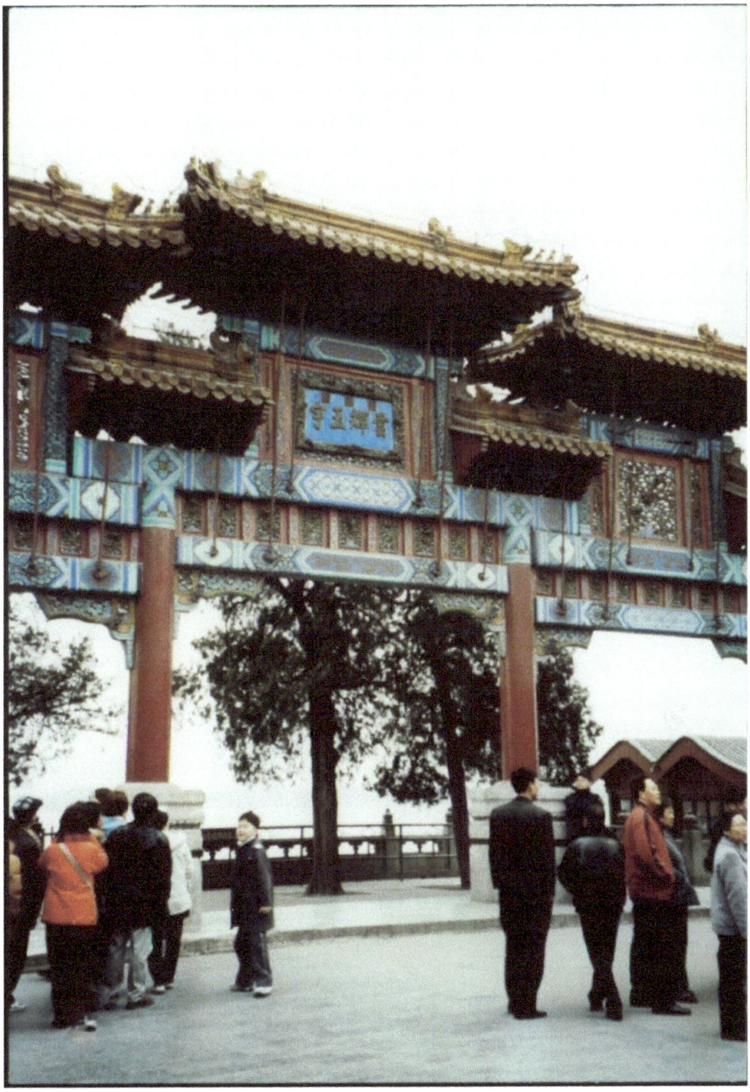

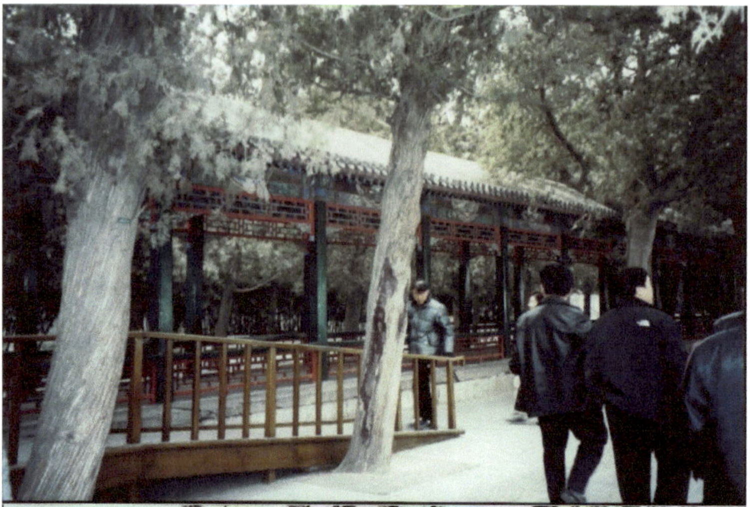

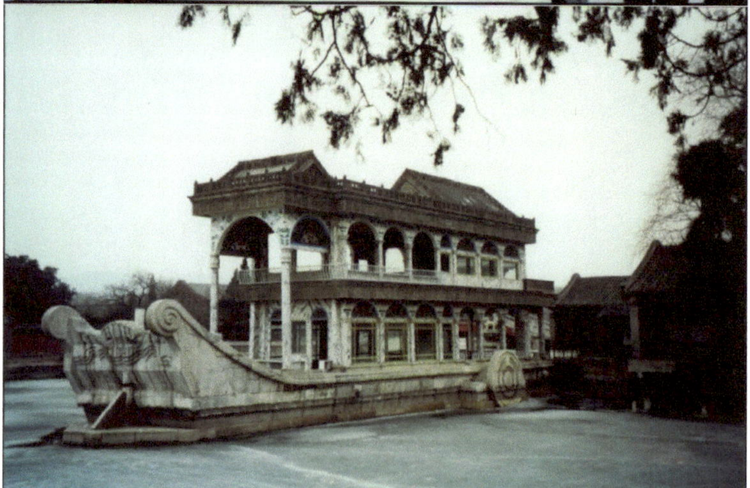

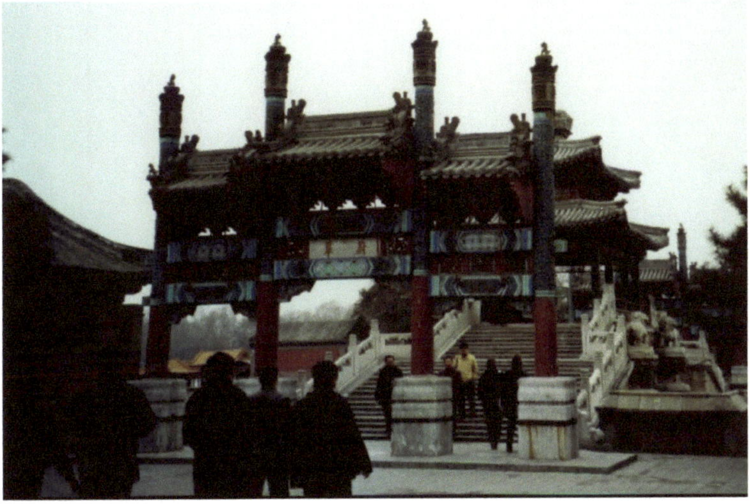

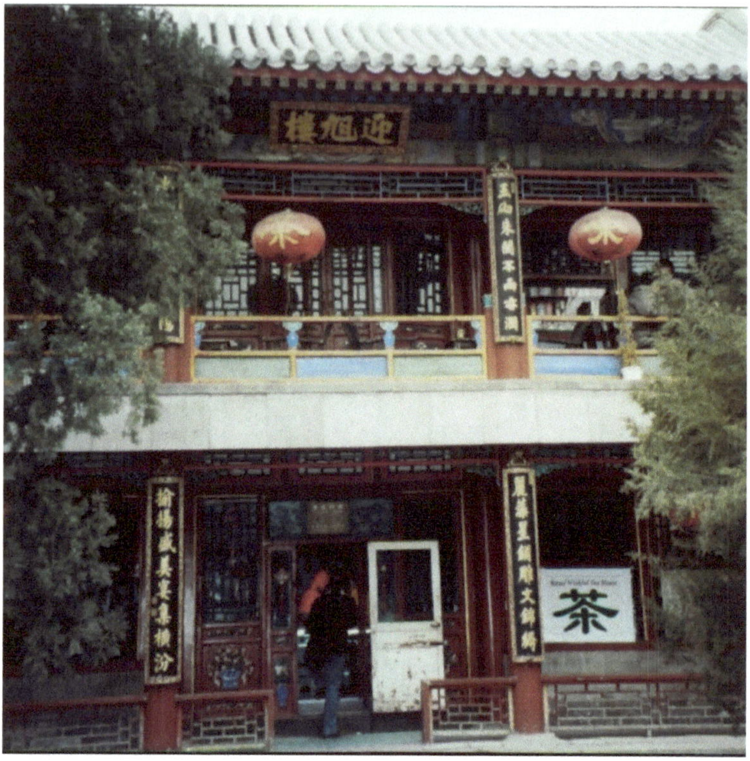
迎旭樓
茶

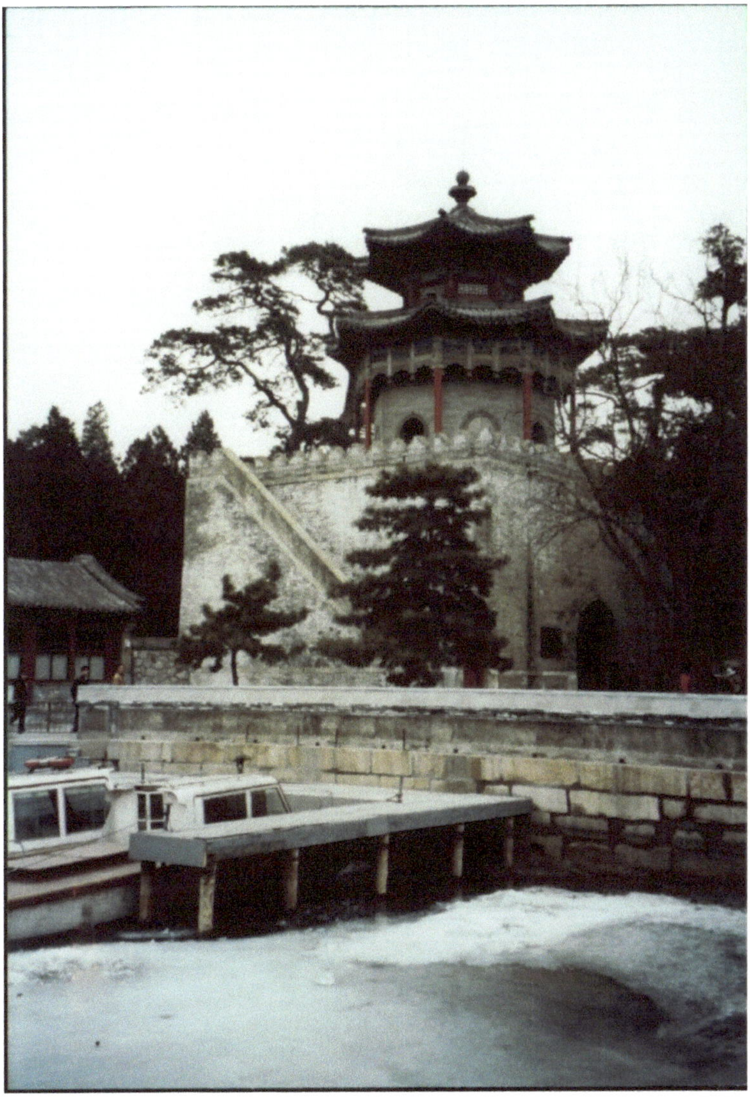

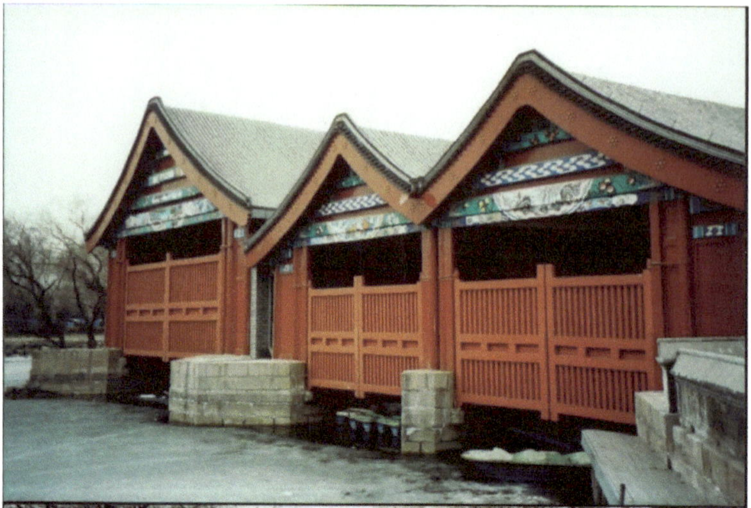

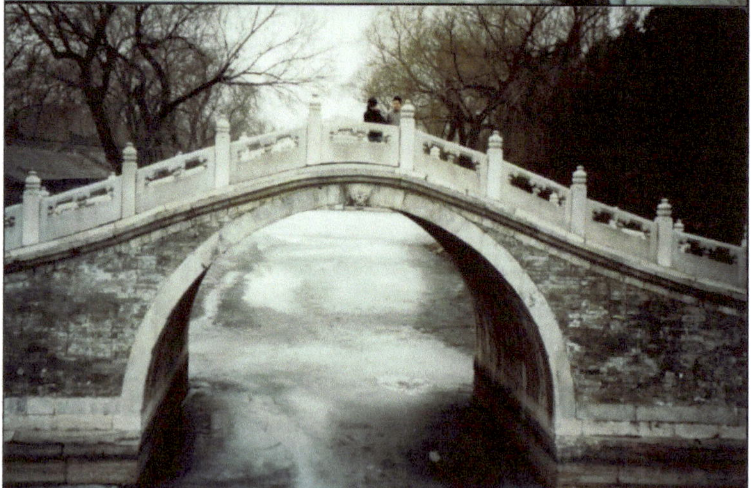

www.ingramcontent.com/pod-product-compliance
Lightning Source LLC
Chambersburg PA
CBHW040918180526
45159CB00002BA/516
* 9 7 8 1 5 1 4 2 9 9 7 5 3 *